Mel Bay's
O'Carolan Harp Tunes
For Mountain Dulcimer
By Shelley Stevens

This book is dedicated to Dr. Susan Porter whose strength and dignity have been an inspiration to all who know her. I am proud to have her for a friend.

Thanks to all my friends who encouraged and supported me through this project, to my family for giving me the freedom to complete it, and to Joyce who started it all.

Computer Graphics by Jan Hall, Ashley, Ohio
Celtic illustrations from the "Book of Kells"
Dover Press—"Celtic Design Coloring Book"
By Ed Sibbett, Jr.

1 2 3 4 5 6 7 8 9 0

Contents

About The Author

Shelley Stevens began music with the piano at an early age and progressed to the classical guitar more than twenty years ago. Upon encountering the Appalachian dulcimer in 1984, the beautiful tonal qualities of the instrument captured her heart and imagination, and became her instrument of choice. As manager and member of the music group *Sweetwater*, Shelley puts all her musical skills to good use performing and giving workshops at venues such as the prestigious Great Black Swamp Dulcimer Festival, the Allegheny Dulcimer Festival, and week-long sessions at Morehead University at Morehead, Kentucky.

Shelley enjoys arranging music for the dulcimer from many genres, such as movie and TV themes, music from the '60s, classical, folk, and Celtic music. The popularity of O'Carolan's music with other instruments inspired Shelley to adapt these lovely tunes to the lap dulcimer. We hope you enjoy it as well.

Shelley Stevens

About the Book

This book is designed for intermediate to advanced level players. Each of these arrangements is tabbed in my own style, but because every person has their own fashion of playing, please feel free to adapt these tunes to your own style and make them your own.

My style is to play a chord, usually at the beginning of a measure, and to let it ring throughout the measure while playing the melody on the melody string. This helps establish a rhythm throughout the piece and works with fingerpicking and flatpicking.

Play only the notes that are marked. Do not strum across all the strings for each note.

I'm a firm advocate of using all the fingers on your left hand (this includes your thumb). I find this increases your speed because you don't have to move your hand so much, and it also broadens the range of notes you can play. For example, in the following measure

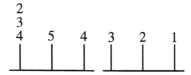

I would form the $\frac{2}{3}$ chord with my middle finger on the 2, my index finger on the 3, and thumb on the 4. Moving my thumb to play the 5, 4, and 3 and using my little finger for the 2 and 1 allows the chord to ring throughout the entire measure and very little hand movement is required. (Thumb plays the melody above the chord and the little finger plays the melody below the chord.)

If you use this fingering technique in playing the arrangements in this book, you will find them very easy. Don't be discouraged by a sore little finger. You will soon develop a callous.

Turlough O'Carolan

Turlough O'Carolan is the most revered of all Ireland's harpers and composers. Born in 1670, he lived most of his life during the oppression of the Irish Catholic people by the penal code which forced them to abandon their religion or be denied their property rights and education possibilities. He never forsook his own people; however he performed and composed for both Irish and English patrons without prejudice, avoiding political or religious controversy in his lyrics.

Blinded by smallpox in his teen years, O'Carolan was befriended by Mrs. MacDermott Roe who became his first patron and who provided him with his first harp and lessons. Starting late in life as a harper, his technique in playing the popular music of the day was not as skilled as was required by patrons of that time and it was suggested that he compose his own music. This change in direction allowed his talents to emerge and brought him fame which has survived for over 250 years.

O'Carolan returned to the house of Mrs. MacDermott Roe in 1738, when he was dying and where he performed his "Farewell to Music" before his death. After a four day wake to which crowds of rich and poor thronged, he was buried in the MacDermott Roe family vault.

Little is known of O'Carolan's personal life. He was the father of seven children by Mary McGuire of County Fermanaugh, and though none of his titled musical works are named for his wife or children, it was his son (also a harper) who published his works in 1748 through a doctor from Dublin University. Unfortunately no complete copy of this book is known to exist, however, there is in the National Library of Dublin a partial copy believed to be one of this 1748 publication.

Most of O'Carolan's music has survived in the form of a one line melody, so we have little knowledge of how he harmonized and chorded his works. This is part of the beauty of his compositions in that each player of O'Carolan's work is free to interpret the accompaniment as he or she feels it.

This book is my interpretation of 30 of O'Carolan's tunes. I hope that you enjoy playing them and will be inspired to learn more of his works. There are over 200 O'Carolan tunes in publication through many sources.

Tunings and Notation

Each piece is written as a melody line in standard notation with 3 or 4 line tablature underneath. Tunings appear at the beginning of each tune. Most are tabbed in 158 (DAD) tuning. Other tunings used are 148 (DGD) and 155♯8 (DAA♯D) chromatic tuning for four equidistant strings. *H* stands for Hammer-on, *P* for Pull-off, *SL* for Slide, ⬨ for Harmonic, *X* means don't play that string, ‖: :‖ means repeat and ⌒ means to hold the note longer than indicated (to add feeling).

Your dulcimer should have a 6 ½ fret which is signified in the tablature as 6+ and should be set up so that you can play 4 strings spaced equally apart. This is for the chromatic tuning.

Chromatic Tuning

This tuning was developed by Janita Baker. It adds a whole new dimension to the lap dulcimer by allowing you to play tunes that were not possible in standard tunings. These arrangements are for fingerpicking only and will require some practice in order to play the tunes without sounding the chromatic string except when necessary. (A good way to practice this is to fingerpick a tune you already know in the 158 tuning while in the 155♯8 tuning.) Other than that this is a straight forward tablature played the same way as any other. For the chromatic tuning I usually fingerpick with my thumb and three fingers (each digit playing its own string). For me this eliminates confusion as to which finger to use for which note.

The Capo

Several tunes in this book require the use of a capo. This changes the mode and the key in which you are playing. Capoing at the first fret puts you into Aeolian, one of the minor modes. When you use a capo, this capoed fret becomes the open tuning which is represented by 0 with the fret number inside (⓪). The rest of the fret numbers remain the same as they would without the capo. If you do not have a capo (available through most dulcimer builders) a large rubber band and a pencil work nicely.

Kitty Magennis

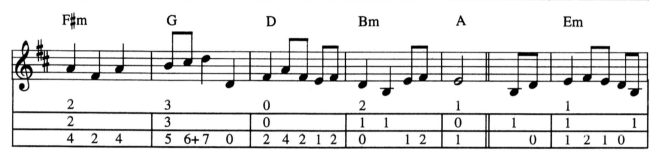

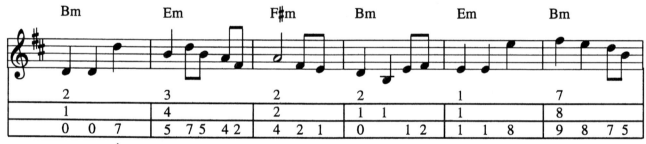

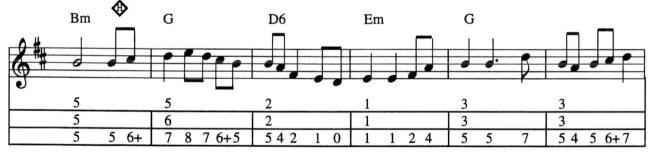

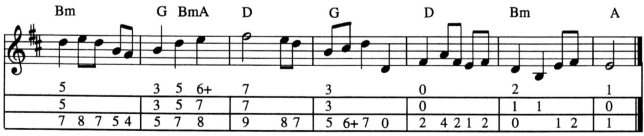

O'Carolans Concerto

A part

O'Carolans Concerto

Lady St. John

(Guitar Capo 2)

8^{va}_____ Play one octave lower

Planxty George Brabazon

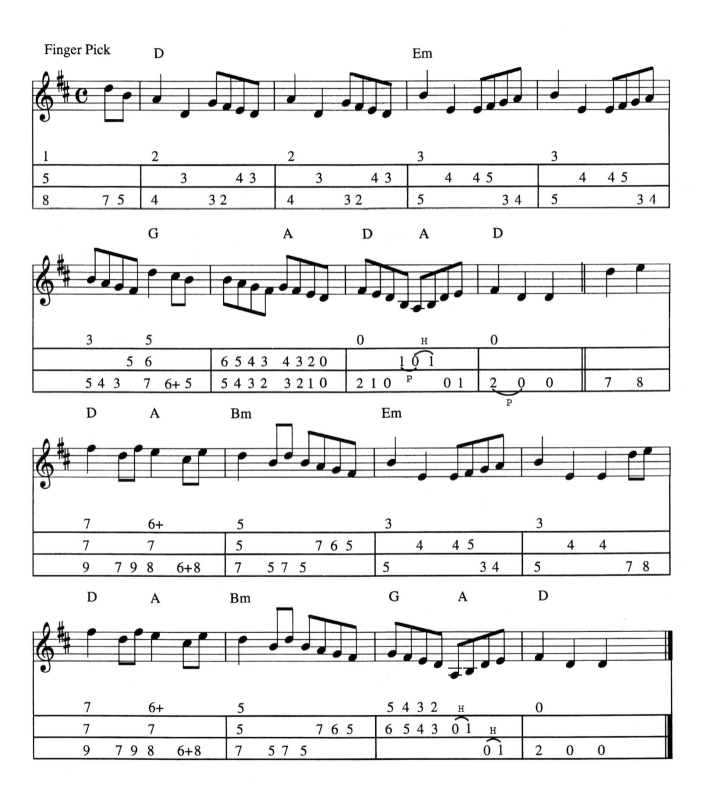

Blind Mary

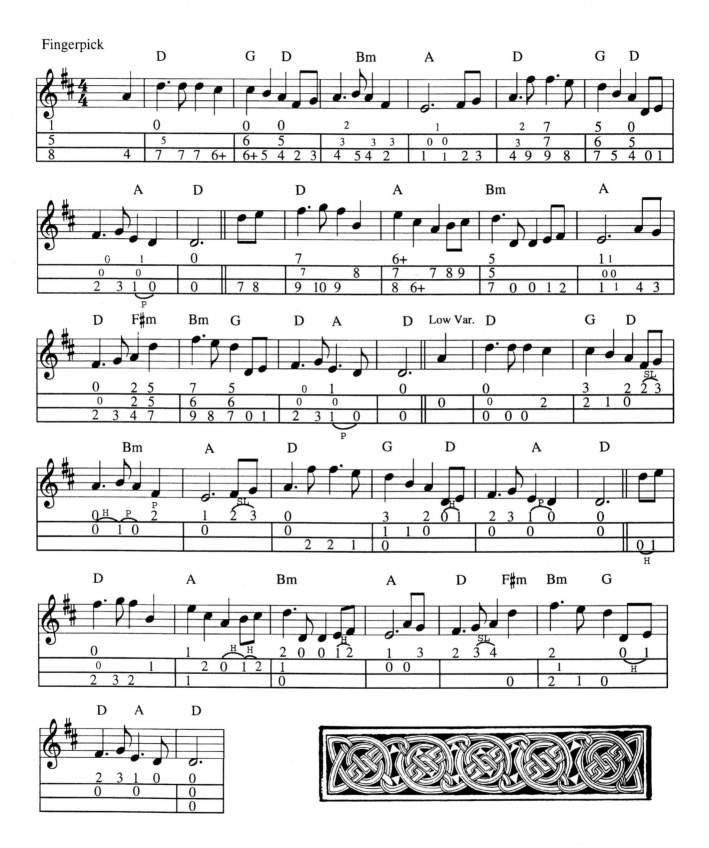

Planxty John Stafford

(Carolan's Receipt)

13

Lord Inchquin

Sheebeg Sheemore

Sir Charles Coote

(Guitar Capo 2)

8va ——— Play one octave lower

Carolans Draught

(Guitar Capo 2)

Miss Murphy

Father Brian MacDermott Roe

Lady Gethin

Peggy Morton

(Guitar Capo 2)

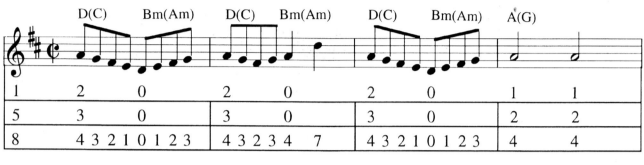

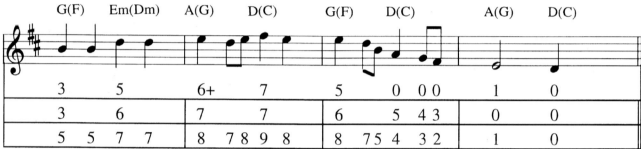

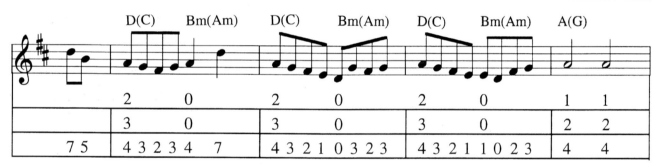

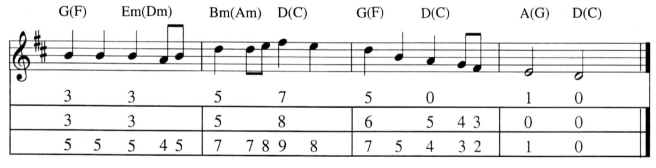

21

Lament for Terence MacDonough

Carolan's Dream

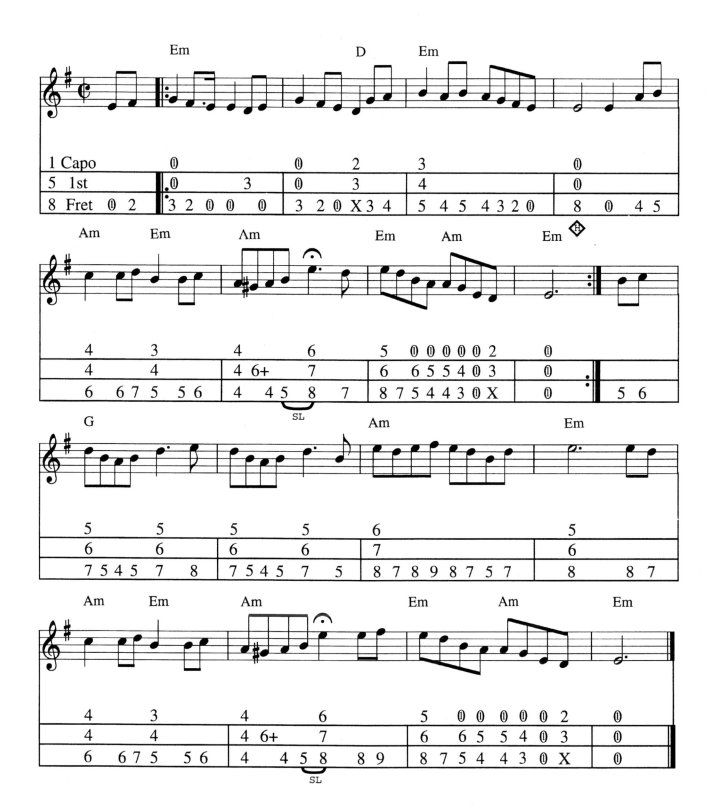

Eleanor Plunkett

Finger Pick

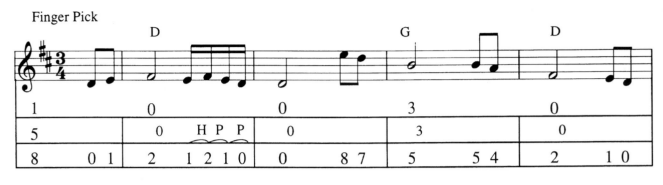

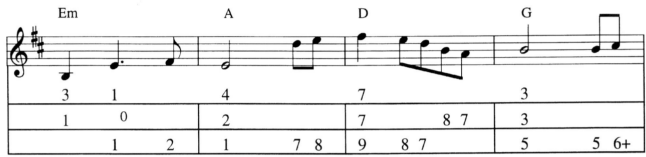

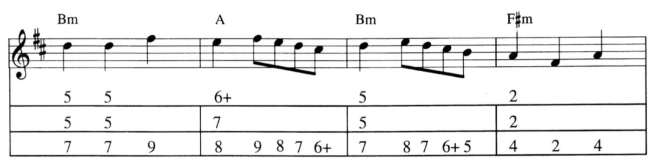

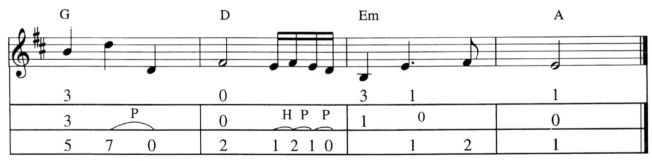

Cremonea

Fingerpick only

Planxty Sweeny

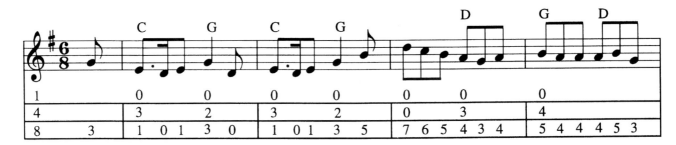

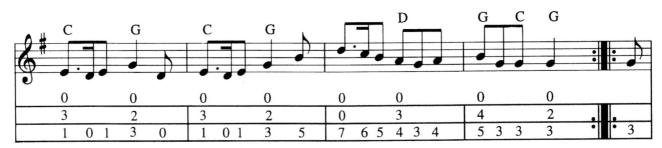

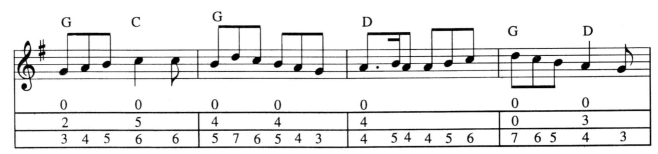

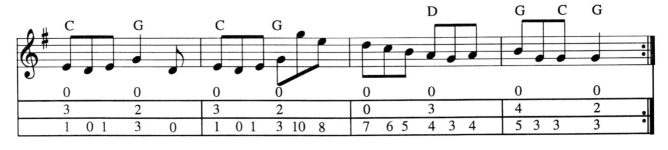

Robert Hawkes

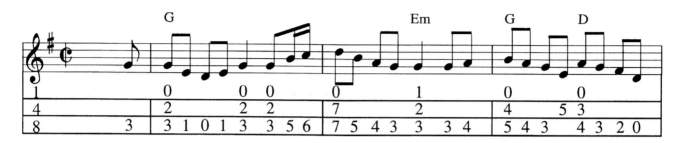

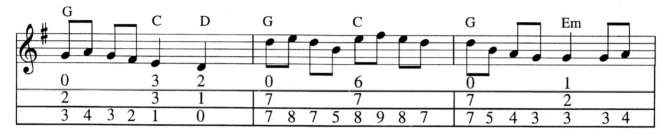

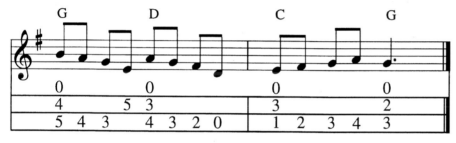

Bridget Cruise

D Mixolydian

Miss Goulding

29

Denis O'Conor

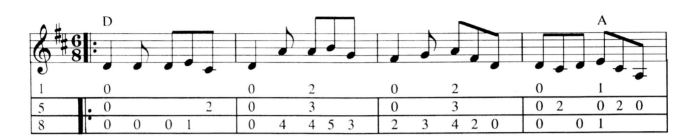

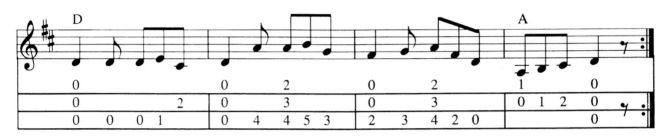

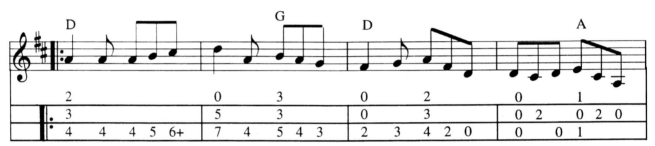

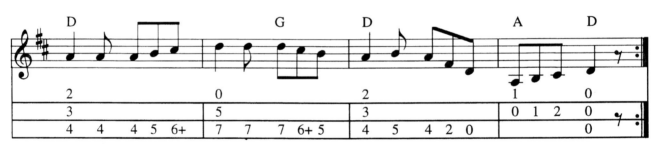

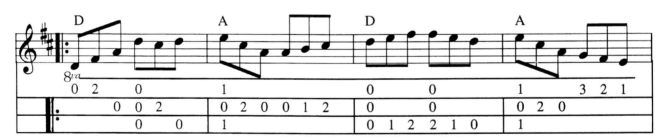

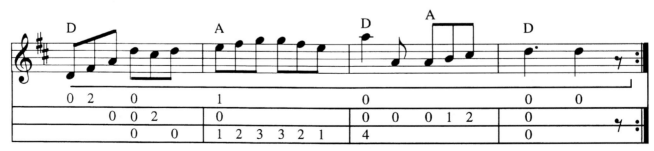

Richard Cusack

Fingerpick only
Mixolydian

The Two William Davises

Squire Parsons

Fingerpick only

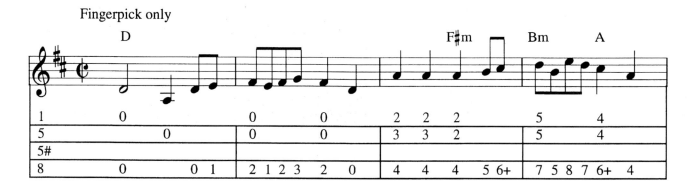

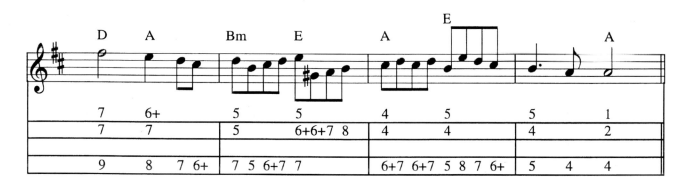

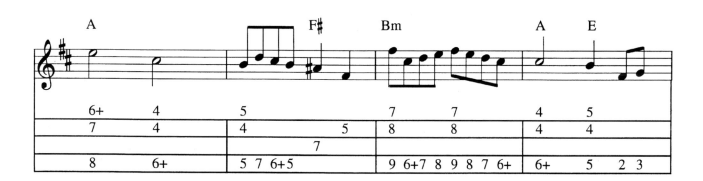

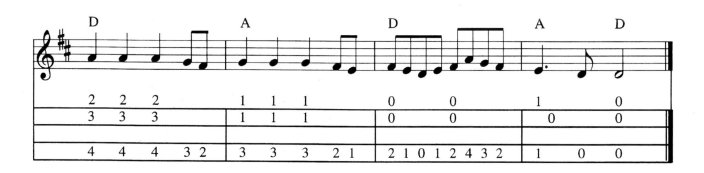

Planxty Drew

Fingerpick

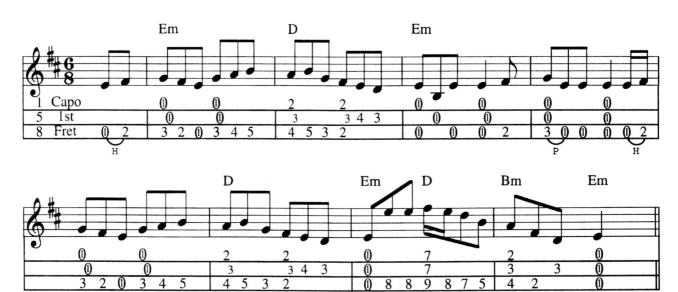

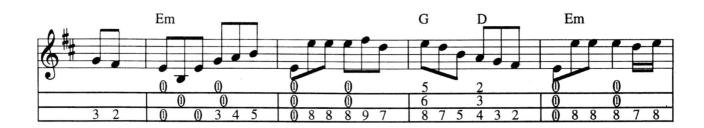

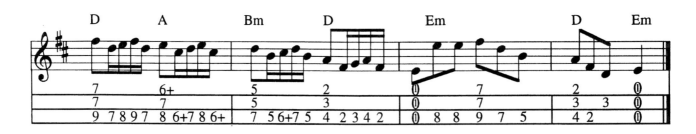

John Drury

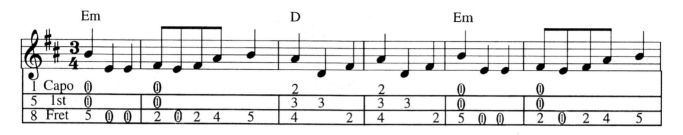

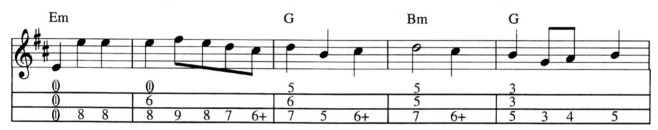

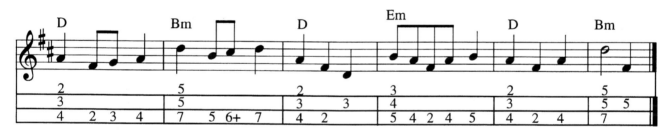

One Bottle More

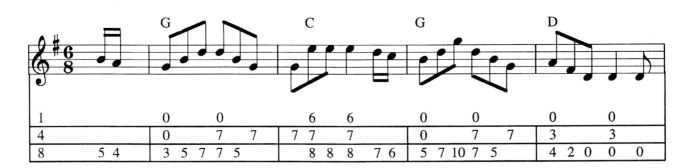

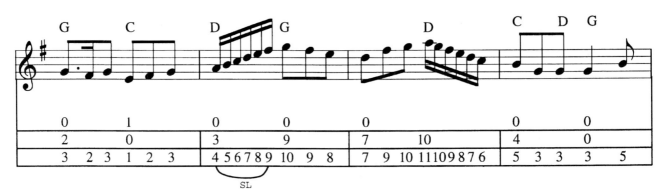

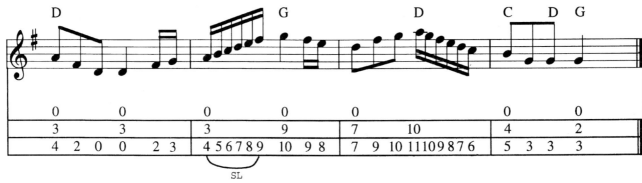

Donal O'Brien

Fingerpick only

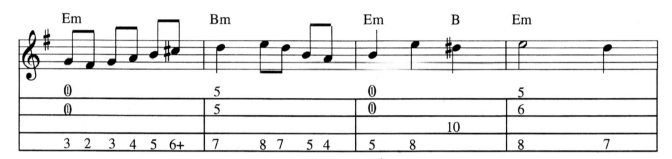

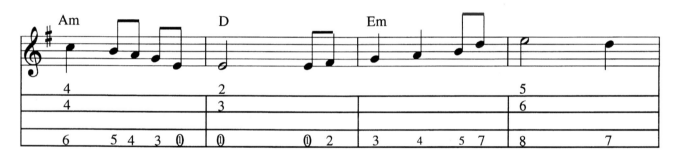

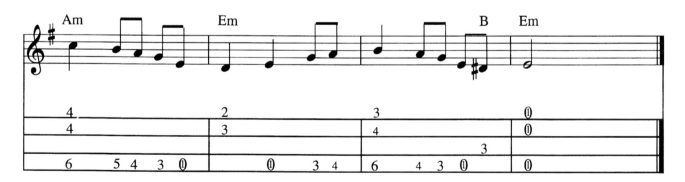

Bibliography

The Harp—its History, Technique and Repertoire
Roslyn Rensch—Praeger Publishers

Modern Ireland—1600 to 1972
R.F. Foster—Allen Lane—The Penguin Press

Oxford Illustrated History of Ireland
R.F. Foster—Oxford University Press

The Complete Works of O'Carolan
Ossian Publications

Great Music at Your Fingertips